ROBOTS

MARK LAMBERT

MACDONALD

Editor Jan Burgess
Designer Peter Luff

Illustrated by:
John Bishop
Robert Burns
Ian Craig
Dan Escott
Ron Hayward
Richard Hook
Eric Jewell & Associates
John Marshall
Peter Robinson
Mike Roffe
Barry Salter
Raymond Turvey

Acknowledgements
Illustrations on page 5 are based on the
BBC television programme *Dr Who*,
courtesy of BBC/Bob Baker and Dave
Martin; BBC/Terry Nation. Illustrations on
pages 24/5 are based on *Dr Who*,
courtesy of BBC/Terence Dicks; *Star
Wars,* courtesy of Lucasfilm U.K. Ltd; the
M.G.M. release *Westworld* ©1973
Metro-Goldwyn-Mayer Inc; the M.G.M.
release *2001: A Space Odyssey* © 1968
Metro-Goldwyn-Mayer Inc.

Our thanks go to the following for their
help in the preparation of this book:
Alderson Research Laboratories Inc.;
British Leyland Cars Limited; British
Olivetti Limited; British Robots
Association; Fiat Auto (U.K.) Limited;
Johns Hopkins University Applied
Physics Laboratory; Hall Automation
Limited; Hawker Siddeley Dynamics
Engineering Limited; Humanoid Systems;
Unimation Inc.; University of Southern
California School of Medicine.

First published in 1981 by
Macdonald Educational Ltd.
Holywell House
Worship Street
London EC2A 2EN

ISBN 0 356 07094 8

Printed in Hong Kong

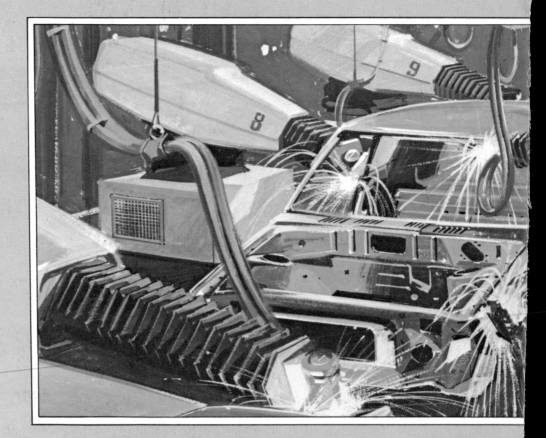

Key to cover

1. Robots have sometimes been built
for fun – to entertain people in
films, on television and at
exhibitions. Alpha performed at the
London Radio Exhibition of 1932.
Find out more about him on page 9.

2. One great advantage of robots is
that they do not need life support
systems. They can therefore be used
in conditions too dangerous for
humans. Consub operates deep under
the oceans. Read more about undersea robots on pages 14 and 15.

3. Shakey can move from place to
place, avoiding obstacles in his
path – no mean feat for a robot!
Find out how on page 27.

4. These Unimate robots weld car
bodies. They are accurate, quick and
never get tired. Turn to pages 12
and 13 for more on factory robots.

5. Robot warriors like these exist only
in the world of films and television.
Read about the real part played by
robots in warfare on pages 18 and 19.

ROBOTS

When most people think about robots, they imagine armies of evil metal monsters, plotting to take over the world. In fact, real-life robots have little to do with science fiction stories. The robots of today are more likely to be doing repetitive factory jobs – welding a car or putting together a piece of machinery. Or they may be working deep under the oceans or far out in space because they can survive in conditions hostile to human beings. Many robots have computer 'brains' and movable 'arms', but they don't have to look anything like a person. So what exactly are robots? How do they differ from other kinds of machine? And why is it that many people are still rather afraid of the whole idea of robots? This book will give you some of the answers to these questions. And if after all you still prefer the robots of *Star Wars* to a car factory welder, you can turn to the back of the book for some ideas on how to make a robot suit to scare your friends.

CONTENTS

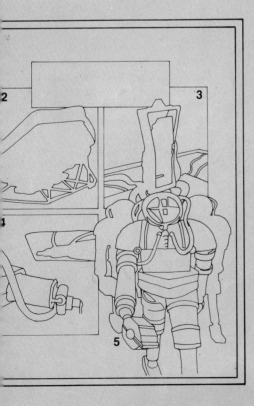

Robot relatives

Several kinds of robot appear in films and books. They differ in the way they are made.

An *android* is a robot that looks exactly like a human. Some are built with mechanical parts. Others are grown from chemicals.

Android

Cyberman

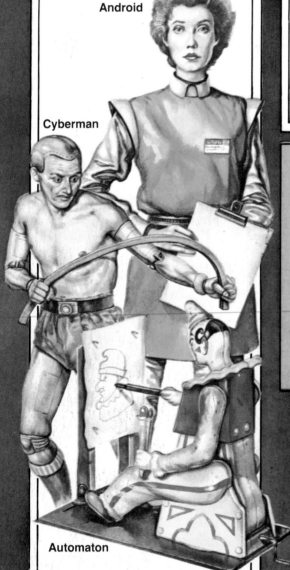

Automaton

A *cyborg* is a robot that is part man and part machine. The Bionic Man, with his bionic arm, bionic legs and bionic eyes, is a cyborg. The Cybermen in *Dr Who* were once human. But gradually all their human parts were replaced. A robot with a human brain is also a cyborg.

An *automaton* is an automatic machine that imitates a human being or any other living thing. Many automata are clockwork toys.

What are Robots?

Many machines that look or act like human beings have appeared in films and books. It is easy to create such robots in stories but these inventions have little to do with reality. However, machines called robots do exist and they are playing a growing part in our lives. It is sometimes difficult to decide whether a particular machine is a robot or not, but there are two questions that you should ask yourself. Does the machine look like a human being? Does it perform human-like actions? If the answer to either question is 'yes', then that machine can be called a robot.

The word 'robot' was first used by the Czechoslovakian writer Karel Čapek (pronounced Chapek). In 1922, he wrote a play called R.U.R. which stands for Rossum's Universal Robots. The play is about a scientist called Rossum who invents an artificial person. A number of such creatures are built, all looking exactly like humans, but without any feelings. Rossum uses his machines as factory workers and so he calls them robots – the word 'robota' in Czech means 'slave-like work'.

Rossum's Universal Robots

In Čapek's play, the robots are made in a factory on a remote island. The factory produces thousands of robots and sells them all over the world. The people who run the factory hope that their robots will make life better by taking over all the boring jobs done by humans.

But the robots are soon used as soldiers. Their human owners make them kill other humans. Eventually, the robots revolt and kill their masters. Only one man is spared but by the end of the play the robots control the whole world.

Robot as enemies

Could robots take over the world? Many robots shown in films and on television act like humans. Some even look like humans. But they do not have the same feelings as humans. They do not laugh or cry. They do not feel pain or pleasure. This may be one reason why many people distrust robots. As a result, in many stories robots are shown as sinister creatures. In the film *Target Earth*, faceless Venusian robots invade our world. The Daleks in *Dr Who* want to exterminate all humans.

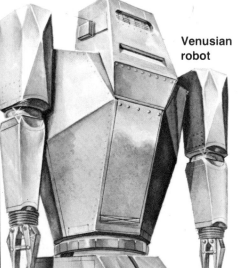

Venusian robot

Daleks

Industrial robot welding arm

In real life, robots are also seen as a threat – to people's jobs. In factories, industrial robots are already beginning to take over some tasks. As this continues, new jobs will have to be found for the humans replaced by robots.

Robots as friends

Isaac Asimov has written stories in which robots are programmed to care for humans. Many other friendly robots have appeared in stories. In the film *Star Wars*, C3PO is a gentle, rather nervous robot. In the television programme, Dr Who's canine (dog-like) friend K9 is his faithful and useful companion.

Robots could become friends in real life, too. Many people would like to have a domestic robot to do the household chores. Arok was built in 1976. It can be programmed to do such things as vacuuming, emptying the rubbish and taking the dog for a walk.

C3PO

K9

AROK

**Organ grinder
(1890)**

As large as life

Long before television and films, clockwork automata entertained people with their lifelike movements. One of the most famous is the Writer. The little boy is life-sized. He dips his quill pen in the ink and writes, following the movements of the pen with his eyes.

The acrobat doll performs tricks, the oarsman can row his little boat on water, and when the organ grinder turns the handle of his music box, the two dancers revolve. Automata like these are now valuable but you can still see them in museums.

**Oarsman
(1900)**

**Writer
(1774)**

**Acrobat
(1876)**

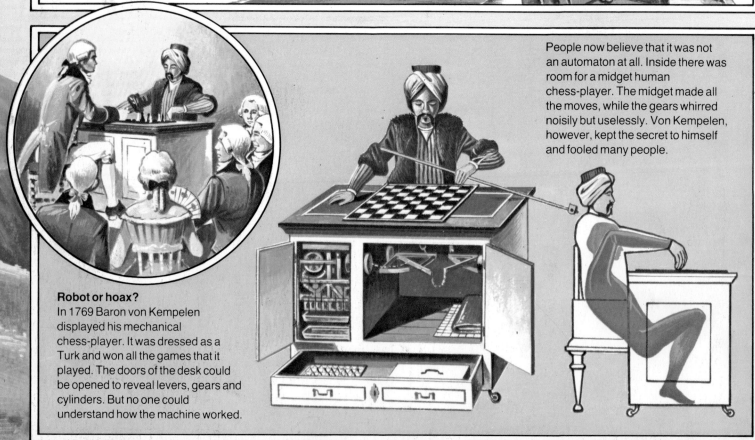

People now believe that it was not an automaton at all. Inside there was room for a midget human chess-player. The midget made all the moves, while the gears whirred noisily but uselessly. Von Kempelen, however, kept the secret to himself and fooled many people.

Robot or hoax?

In 1769 Baron von Kempelen displayed his mechanical chess-player. It was dressed as a Turk and won all the games that it played. The doors of the desk could be opened to reveal levers, gears and cylinders. But no one could understand how the machine worked.

Machines that look like People

People have always been fascinated by the idea of machines that look or behave like humans. There were stories of such machines long before they could actually be built. Hephaestus, the Greek god of fire, was said to have created a brass giant called Talus. In about AD 60 Hero of Alexandria built a mechanical man out of jade (a semi-precious rock). Centuries later, in the 1700s and 1800s, people made many ingenious machines called automata. They looked like humans and could write, walk, play music, and some could even talk. Automata were operated by clockwork mechanisms inside them.

The human body is highly complex and there are still many unanswered questions about the way it works. The idea of a mechanical person is perhaps rather frightening but despite this, scientists might one day succeed in making a realistic copy of a human being.

The first robot
The Ancient Greeks made up stories about their gods. They believed that Hephaestus was the god of fire or the blacksmith god. His forge was in a volcano on the island of Lemnos. Hephaestus made a huge giant out of brass, called Talus. Talus guarded the island of Crete by heating up his body and hugging any intruders to death.

Robot toys

Robot toys are enjoyed by both children and adults. Some toy robots are copies of robots that appear in films. Others are purely imaginary. Nearly all toy robots can perform some kind of action such as walking along or firing a 'ray gun'. Some of the early toy robots have even become collector's pieces.

Although they may not look like it at first sight, all the robots on these two pages are toys because they are designed to entertain people.

Performing Robots

In the early 1900s, science fiction stories about robots became very popular. As a result performing robots were used to attract people to exhibitions and fairs. These robots were made to look like the robots that, until this time, had only been described in stories. The automata of the 1800s look more like dolls.

One of the first performing robots was Eric, built in 1928 by Captain W. H. Richards. At the opening of the Model Engineer Society, Eric was asked to make a speech. He rose to his feet and bowed. His eyes flashed and sparks flew across his teeth. Then he looked to right and left and began to speak. Eric's movements were controlled by two battery-powered motors, but his speech was actually delivered by someone speaking into a microphone offstage.

Tourist guide and rocket robot

ONOFF lives in the Wonders of the World Museum in California. He hands out pictures of himself and, with lights flashing, guides visitors to the museum's large collection of toy robots. Cosmos appeared at the Land and Cosmos Exhibition in Paris in 1958. He was radio-controlled and rode about on a 'rocket car' waving his arms and opening and closing his mouth.

ONOFF

Cosmos

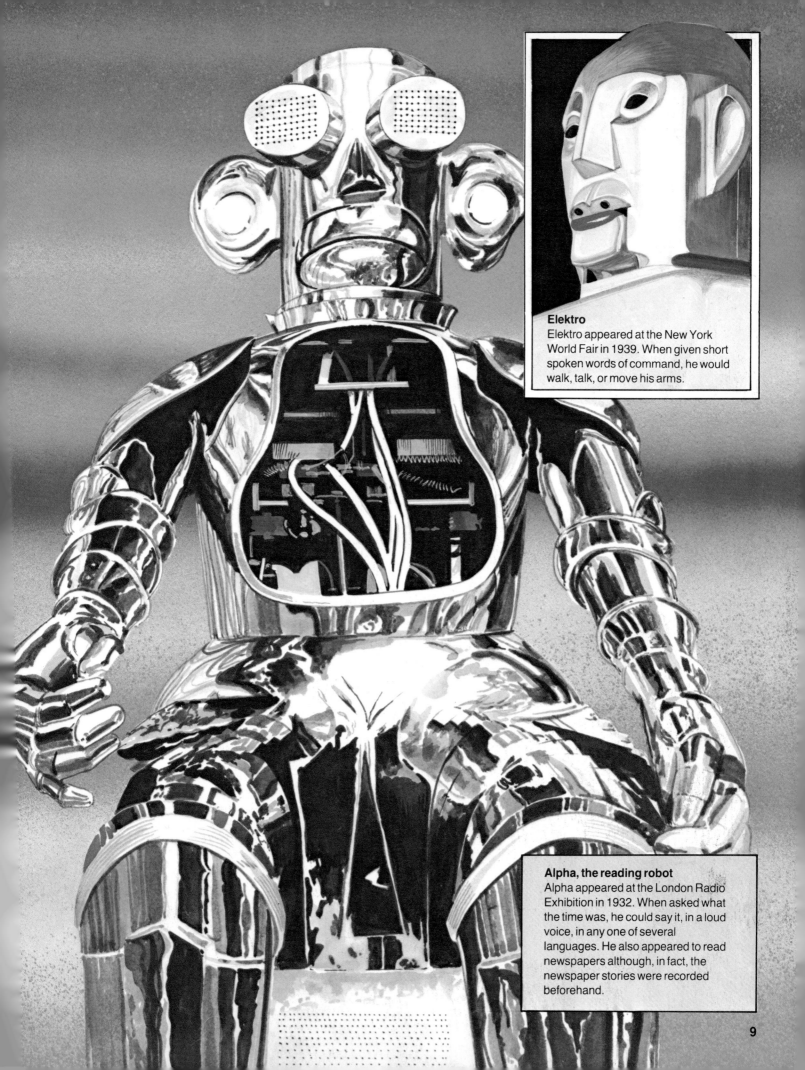

Elektro
Elektro appeared at the New York World Fair in 1939. When given short spoken words of command, he would walk, talk, or move his arms.

Alpha, the reading robot
Alpha appeared at the London Radio Exhibition in 1932. When asked what the time was, he could say it, in a loud voice, in any one of several languages. He also appeared to read newspapers although, in fact, the newspaper stories were recorded beforehand.

From Machine to Robot

Robots imitate humans. But are robots just machines or do they have any special characteristics that make them more like human beings? To answer this question, think of the wide variety of things that you can do compared with a machine. One reason you can do so much is that you have a brain that can learn and make decisions. By using eyes, ears, nose and touch you sense what is going on around you. This information is 'fed back' to your brain and influences what you do next.

This system is called feedback. A machine generally does not have feedback. It can do only one or two jobs according to instructions, and it cannot think for itself. For a machine to be a true robot, it must have senses, and a brain to process the information that the senses feed back to it.

Automatic machines
An automatic washing machine carries out a series of instructions — fill, heat, wash, rinse, spin-dry. It has simple feedback devices, for example, the thermostat that switches off the heater. But it is not a robot because it has no brain, only simple electronic circuits.

Human-like robots?
A robot which is built for a special purpose can probably do its job better if it does not look human. Robots that are not human-like can be faster, stronger and more accurate than humans. In this scene from the future one of the robots is quite like a human, though most robots look quite different. The only sort of machine which needs to look like a human is one which is built to do exactly the same things as humans can do.

How feedback works
A feedback device controls the output of a machine (what the machine does). It detects changes caused by the output and sends this information back to the machine. This makes the machine behave differently.

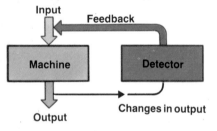

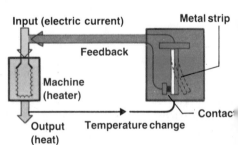

▲ A thermostat is a feedback device. It reacts to changes in temperature. If the water gets too hot, the metal strip bends away from the contact and breaks the electrical circuit. When the water cools down, the thermostat switches on again.

A robot brain

The 'brain' of a robot is called a computer. The robot is 'taught' by programming its computer. The program is a set of instructions that tells the computer what to do with the information it receives from the robot's 'eyes', 'ears' or other sensors.

The program and other information are fed into the input unit and stored in the memory. The instructions are carried out by the calculating unit. The control unit controls the whole computer, and it also directs the output signals to the various parts of the robot.

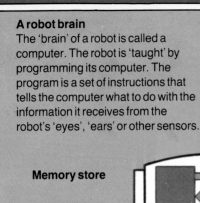

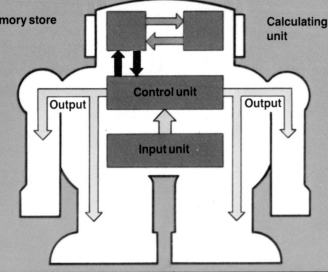

Memory store

Calculating unit

Output

Control unit

Output

Input unit

Tiny electronic circuits

Computers were once very large, but modern electronic circuits can be made up on tiny pieces of silicon, or silicon chips. A single silicon chip can contain hundreds of transistors and other electrical parts.

Robot pilot

An autopilot keeps an aircraft on course and helps it land. Several feedback devices send information to a computer brain, and this brain operates the aircraft controls. An autopilot is therefore a simple robot.

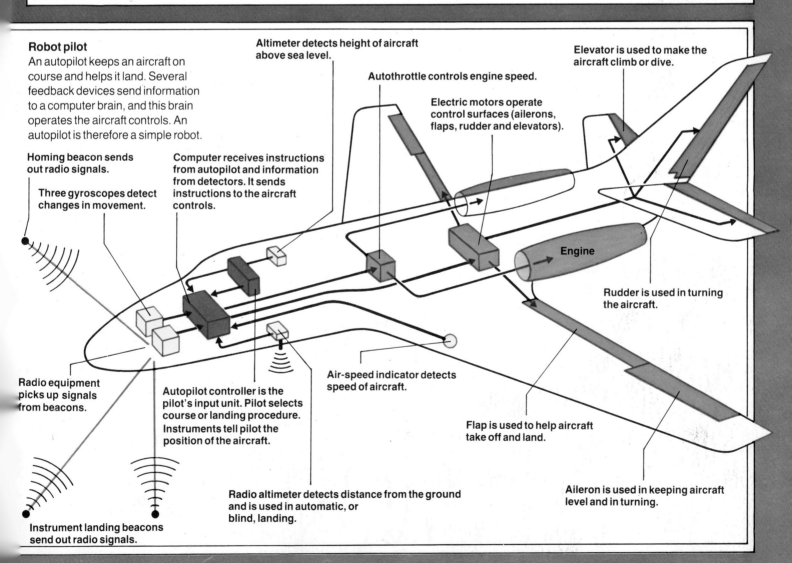

Altimeter detects height of aircraft above sea level.

Autothrottle controls engine speed.

Electric motors operate control surfaces (ailerons, flaps, rudder and elevators).

Elevator is used to make the aircraft climb or dive.

Homing beacon sends out radio signals.

Three gyroscopes detect changes in movement.

Computer receives instructions from autopilot and information from detectors. It sends instructions to the aircraft controls.

Engine

Rudder is used in turning the aircraft.

Radio equipment picks up signals from beacons.

Autopilot controller is the pilot's input unit. Pilot selects course or landing procedure. Instruments tell pilot the position of the aircraft.

Air-speed indicator detects speed of aircraft.

Flap is used to help aircraft take off and land.

Instrument landing beacons send out radio signals.

Radio altimeter detects distance from the ground and is used in automatic, or blind, landing.

Aileron is used in keeping aircraft level and in turning.

Hand-built by robots

A motor car factory is an ideal place to use robots. Cars move along a production line. They pass a series of 'stations' and at each station a particular job is done.

In some car factories Unimate robots have taken over nearly all the welding jobs (joining two pieces of metal by melting them together). First the four body panels are clamped together in a 'gate'. Robots weld the body panels and the gate is lifted away. The body then passes down the line to more welding robots (as shown here). By the end of the line about 400 welds have been applied.

The whole production line is controlled by a central computer. A single robot welding line may soon produce as many as 1,000 car bodies per day.

Mobot

Mobot is a remote-controlled manipulator designed for use in radioactive areas. It is operated by a human controller who sits in safety outside the danger area. However, like industrial robots, Mobot can be programmed to perform a series of actions over and over again. Mobot can handle extremely delicate objects, such as glass containers. It also has 'eyes' and 'ears' that keep the operator informed about what is happening – television cameras are mounted on two movable arms, and there are microphones on the 'wrists'.

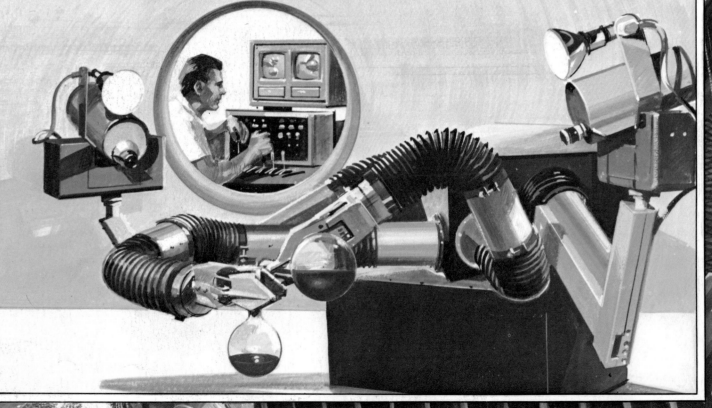

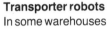

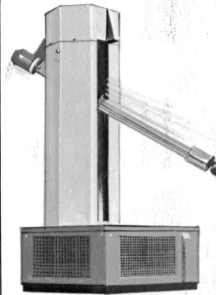

Transporter robots

In some warehouses and factories, robot transporters are used to carry materials from place to place. These wheeled robots are controlled by a central computer. They can be guided by overhead or underfloor wires, or they may have 'eyes' that follow white lines painted on the floor.

Robots in Industry

A robot used in a modern factory is not at all like a science-fiction robot. Its only human-like characteristics are a brain and an arm, but these are all it needs to do its work. The brain, or computer, is programmed so that the robot arm performs a certain series of actions. These robots are used for welding, painting, loading sacks onto trolleys and other simple tasks. At the present time, an industrial robot does not have feedback, but it does have one important advantage over an automatic machine. Its computer brain can be reprogrammed quickly and easily so that the arm performs a new set of actions. A welding, painting or loading robot cannot do its job as accurately as a person, so such robots are used for heavy, dirty or unpleasant jobs. Recently, however, robots have been developed that can make very precise movements. They can position things to within 0.1mm, so they are used to assemble small parts. The next step is to give such robots feedback. For this they will need 'eyes' and a sense of touch.

Painting by robot

A robot can be 'trained' to paint car bodies. First the robot's computer is switched to 'learn'. Then a human operator uses the robot arm to paint a car. As he does this, all the movements he makes are fed into the computer's memory. When one car body has been painted, the computer is switched to 'perform'. All by itself, the robot arm paints the next car; and the next; and the next . . .

Underwater robot eye

Looking like a flying saucer, Smartie dives beneath the waves to inspect underwater structures such as pipelines and the supports of oil platforms. Its television cameras can see even in very dark or murky water. Smartie stands for submarine automatic remote television inspection equipment. It is controlled by an operator on the surface and receives its instructions via a cable. Its computer automatically keeps it level in the water, and powerful thrusters enable it to hover even when there are strong currents.

Smartie

Walking on the bottom

Japanese engineers are now working on an unmanned submersible that can walk on the sea bed. As well as thrusters, it will have six legs, like some kind of gigantic underwater insect. The legs will make it very stable, whether it is walking on rock, sand or mud. Its manipulators will enable it to carry out construction work, and it will be possible to leave it on the bottom for weeks at a time.

Undersea Robots

Divers have to be sent down to work under the sea wearing diving suits or in submersibles. At great depths or in bad weather it may be too dangerous for divers, but remote-controlled submersibles can often be used instead. They are linked to a control room on the surface by a cable. A controller 'drives' the submersible and operates its manipulators, using underwater television cameras to see what he is doing. Because they are remote-controlled, submersibles like these are not true robots. However, one day, the operator may well be replaced by a computer, and a true underwater robot will be able to dive down, see what the situation is, and decide for itself what to do.

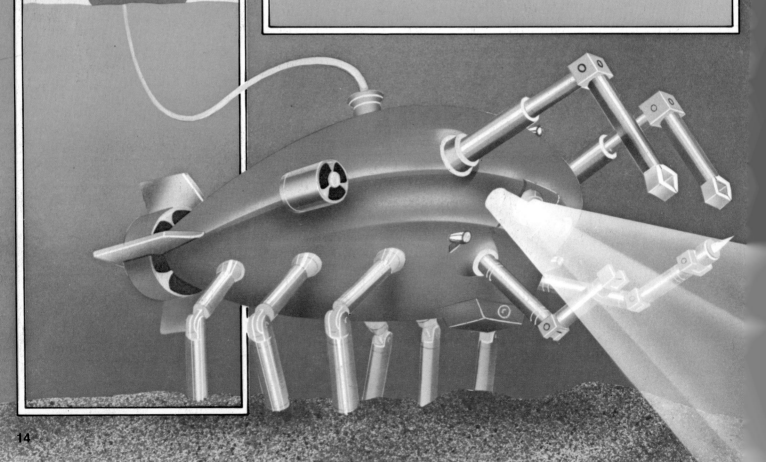

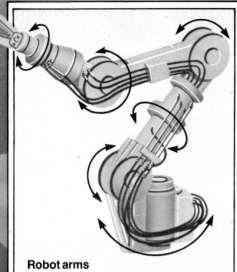

Robot arms

Unmanned submersibles and industrial robots have one important thing in common. They both have mechanical arms, or manipulators. A robot arm has several joints. Each joint allows movement in one particular direction. This combination of joints allows the whole arm, together with its 'hand', to move in any direction.

The future of undersea robots

Eventually, undersea robots will be able to move about without cables. Unlike human divers, they do not need air so they will be able to stay underwater for a long time and go almost anywhere. With such robots we will be able to explore the deepest parts of the oceans. As more food for people and livestock is needed, robots could also be used to help farm fish, shellfish and seaweed crops.

Working underwater

▶ Consub can be used to perform several tasks. Television cameras are used for inspection work, and its powerful manipulators drill rock samples, clean equipment and make repairs. Consub can travel through the water, hover, or rest firmly on the sea bed. The operator sits in the control room on board ship. From there he controls all the actions of the submersible and keeps track on where it is.

Consub

Robots in Space

Robots have played an important part in space exploration. The first moon landing was by a robot spacecraft. Astronauts only followed once the robots proved it to be possible. Some places are too dangerous for humans to go. In these cases only robots can be used. For example, in 1972 the Russian probe Luna 20 collected rock samples from a mountainous region of the Moon. Luna 18 had crashed there in 1971. It only takes about three days to get to the Moon, but many flights are far too long to send humans. The American spacecraft Voyager 1 took 18 months to reach Jupiter. Pioneer 10 will take 1,700,000 years to reach the star Aldabaran!

Another robot spacecraft was the Russian space-ferry Progress 1. It carried out the first automatic docking, linking up with the Salyut 6/Soyuz 27 space station, and bringing supplies to the two men on board.

Voyage to the outer planets

On 5 March 1979, Voyager 1 passed within 280,000 km of Jupiter. Its television cameras sent back amazingly detailed pictures of the swirling red whirlpools in the planet's atmosphere. The spacecraft then swung round Jupiter to arrive near Saturn in November 1980. Voyager 2 was launched to reach Saturn in 1981. From there it may go on to Uranus and possibly Neptune.

Lunokhod Moon rovers

The two Russian Lunokhods were directed from Earth by remote control. Lunokhod 1 landed in November 1970. Lunokhod 2 (shown here) landed in January 1973 and travelled 37 km. Both rovers sent back television pictures and scientific information. To recharge its battery, a Lunokhod lifted its lid, exposing its solar cells to the Sun.

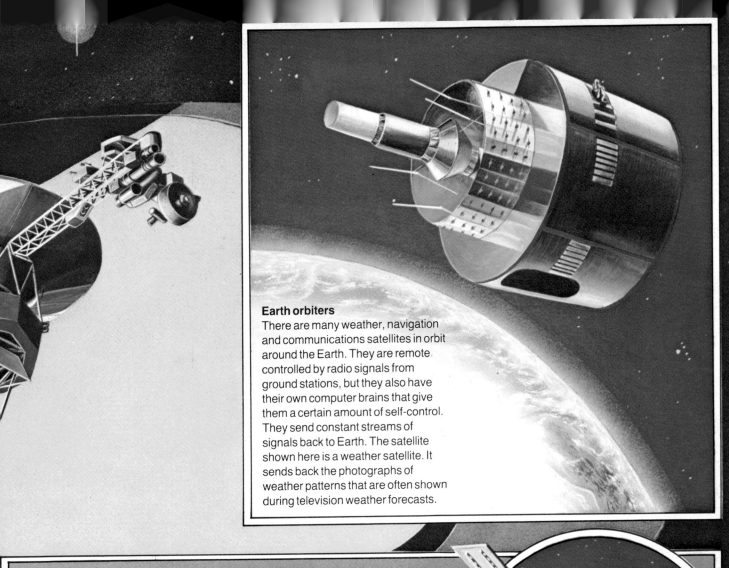

Earth orbiters

There are many weather, navigation and communications satellites in orbit around the Earth. They are remote controlled by radio signals from ground stations, but they also have their own computer brains that give them a certain amount of self-control. They send constant streams of signals back to Earth. The satellite shown here is a weather satellite. It sends back the photographs of weather patterns that are often shown during television weather forecasts.

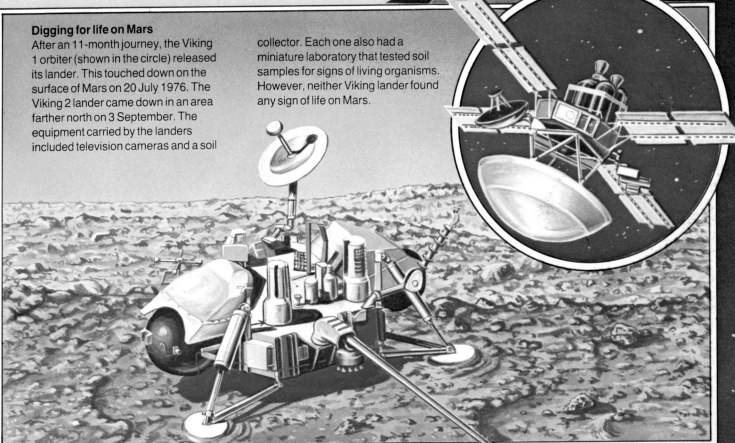

Digging for life on Mars

After an 11-month journey, the Viking 1 orbiter (shown in the circle) released its lander. This touched down on the surface of Mars on 20 July 1976. The Viking 2 lander came down in an area farther north on 3 September. The equipment carried by the landers included television cameras and a soil collector. Each one also had a miniature laboratory that tested soil samples for signs of living organisms. However, neither Viking lander found any sign of life on Mars.

War in space

Wars fought on other planets still belong only to science fiction stories. But war in space may begin sooner than we think. There are now many spy satellites circling the Earth. With special cameras they can take detailed pictures of the ground. Some people suggest that killer satellites could soon be used to knock out these spies, using such devices as laser beams.

Cruise missiles

A cruise missile flies to its target at tree-top height, avoiding enemy radar. It is guided by a computer program that is continually being updated and directs it round known enemy defence positions. The missile finds its way by matching the land below with its program. It is very accurate and can land within a few metres of its target.

Robot bomb detector

The British Army uses a remote-controlled device called Wheelbarrow to detect booby traps. If the soldiers suspect that a bomb has been planted in a car, Wheelbarrow is sent in to investigate. Its television camera sends back pictures to the controllers and it also has a number of devices for de-fusing bombs. This robot saves human lives. If a bomb does go off, only the robot is damaged.

Guided missiles

Unlike bullets, guided missiles do not have to be aimed accurately. They are fitted with detectors that seek out the target automatically. A missile with infra-red detectors can home in on the heat created by an enemy aircraft's engine. Other missiles are guided by radar, laser beams or television.

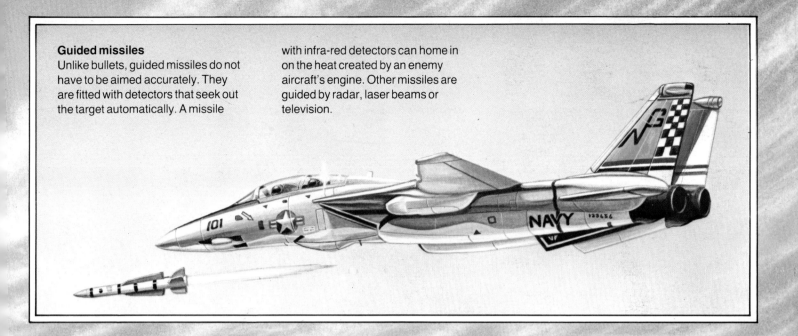

Robots at War

The first missiles used in war were stones, rocks, arrows and spears. But as technology developed, more powerful missiles, such as bullets and shells, were invented. Today, huge rocket-powered missiles can be fired from one continent to another. These missiles have to be aimed, otherwise they would not hit their targets. However, new missiles have been designed which are, in fact, robots and can aim themselves. Guided missiles home in on their targets automatically. Cruise missiles use computer brains to find their way to their targets. Other robots include remote-controlled aircraft which are used for bombing, air-to-air combat and to spy out enemy territory. The Sting Ray is a robot torpedo. It can be dropped from a helicopter and homes in on the sound of a ship's engine. Its computer brain can even tell the difference between enemy ships and friendly ones.

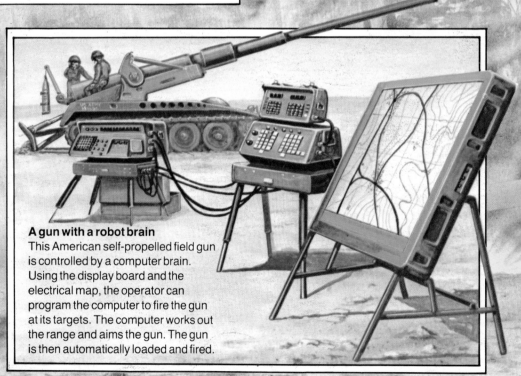

Tomorrow's army?

More and more weapons are becoming automatic and remote controlled. In a few years robot tanks and other war machines might be invented, so why not robot soldiers too?

In the event of robot soldiers being used, humans would still have to control them. It is unlikely, therefore, that robots would ever fight wars alone.

A gun with a robot brain

This American self-propelled field gun is controlled by a computer brain. Using the display board and the electrical map, the operator can program the computer to fire the gun at its targets. The computer works out the range and aims the gun. The gun is then automatically loaded and fired.

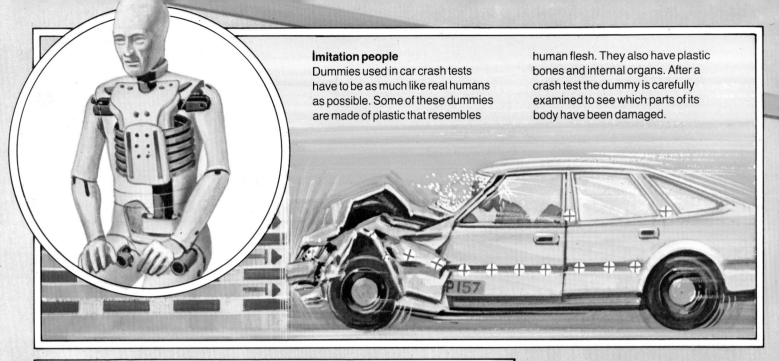

Imitation people

Dummies used in car crash tests have to be as much like real humans as possible. Some of these dummies are made of plastic that resembles human flesh. They also have plastic bones and internal organs. After a crash test the dummy is carefully examined to see which parts of its body have been damaged.

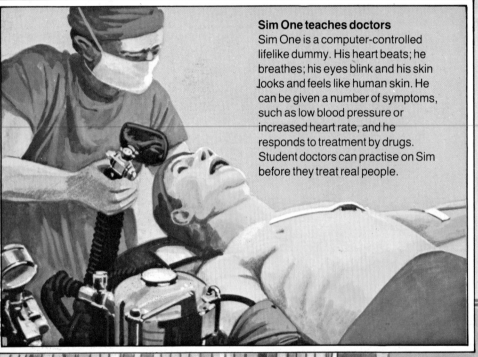

Sim One teaches doctors

Sim One is a computer-controlled lifelike dummy. His heart beats; he breathes; his eyes blink and his skin looks and feels like human skin. He can be given a number of symptoms, such as low blood pressure or increased heart rate, and he responds to treatment by drugs. Student doctors can practise on Sim before they treat real people.

Elsie the robot tortoise

Elsie feeds on electricity and likes to keep her batteries fully charged. The recharger is positioned inside her hutch. Elsie is attracted towards the recharger by a light. Every time she touches an obstacle in the way she moves away and tries again until eventually she gets there.

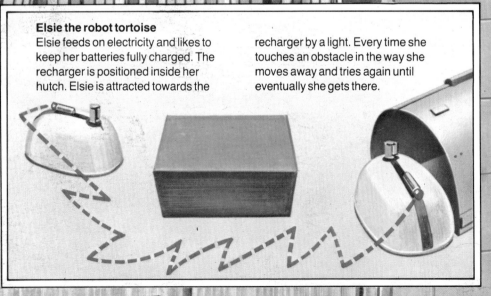

Robot Teachers

The computer brains of robots are really just high-speed calculating machines. Humans have to teach them what to do. But if robots ever become intelligent, they may begin to teach us. Even now there are robot-like machines that are used to provide us with information. Some schools have their own computers to help pupils work out complicated problems. Leachim is a teaching robot with a computer brain. It was built in 1973 by Dr Michael J. Freeman in New York (the name Leachim is almost Michael spelled backwards).

Even models of the human body can provide valuable information. Realistic dummies are used to find out how car crashes and invisible rays affect people. Sim One is a realistic dummy used in teaching medicine to student doctors. Not all teaching robots are human-like, however. Robot tortoises and robot mice have also been built which imitate the actions of real animals. Scientists use them to find out more about how living creatures behave.

Leachim, the robot teacher
Leachim is used to teach children of about 10 years old. The pupil first dials his code number. Leachim recognises the pupil and the lesson can begin. Leachim asks the pupil a question and waits. The pupil then dials the answer and Leachim tells him whether it is right or wrong. Each lesson lasts about 15 minutes and at the end of a lesson Leachim adds up the numbers of right and wrong answers. He then tells the pupil what he must study in order to do better next time. Leachim can teach several subjects including science, maths and history.

Testing invisible rays safely
Some kinds of invisible ray, or radiation, can be dangerous. If people take in too much they are harmed. Plastic test dummies have been built in America containing artificial organs that react just like the real ones. They are used to find out what happens when people come into contact with different levels of radiation.

Part Human, Part Robot

People can live quite easily despite losing one or more parts of their bodies. Although it is very sad when someone loses an arm or a leg, these parts can often be replaced. The first artificial limbs were made in the 1500s in France, but they were heavy and awkward. Today there are several kinds of artificial arm that work very well. Some are operated by the person's own muscles; others are powered by electricity or compressed gas. Some are even operated by small computers. Scientists are learning to replace more and more human parts so perhaps some day there will be a real Bionic Man.

There are other ways in which machines can make the human body work more efficiently. Scientists are developing a walking shell – a robot in which a paralysed person can walk. And anyone operating the CAMS walking lorry or Hardiman really becomes part of a very powerful machine.

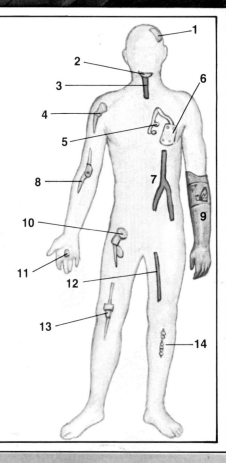

Finger-tip control
The experimental Collins hand, made in 1961, feels exactly like a human hand. The main grip is between the thumb and first finger.

Spare parts
Replacement parts have to be made of materials that the body will not reject, such as plastic or stainless steel. Here are some of the spare parts now available:
1. Skull plate (metal, bone)
2. Lower jaw (silicone)
3. Wind-pipe (rubber)
4. Upper arm bone (metal)
5. Heart valves (plastic, fibre)
6. Heart pacemaker
7. Large artery (plastic)
8. Elbow joint (metal)
9. Arm and hand
10. Hip joint (metal)
11. Knuckle joint (metal)
12. Small vein (woven plastic)
13. Knee joint (metal)
14. Shin-bone support (metal)

Almost as good as new
Extremely efficient artificial hands have already been designed. They are strong but can also be used very precisely. Some even seem to give a sense of touch so that their wearers can handle delicate objects even when blindfolded. Perhaps one day artificial limbs will be designed that are just as good as the real thing.

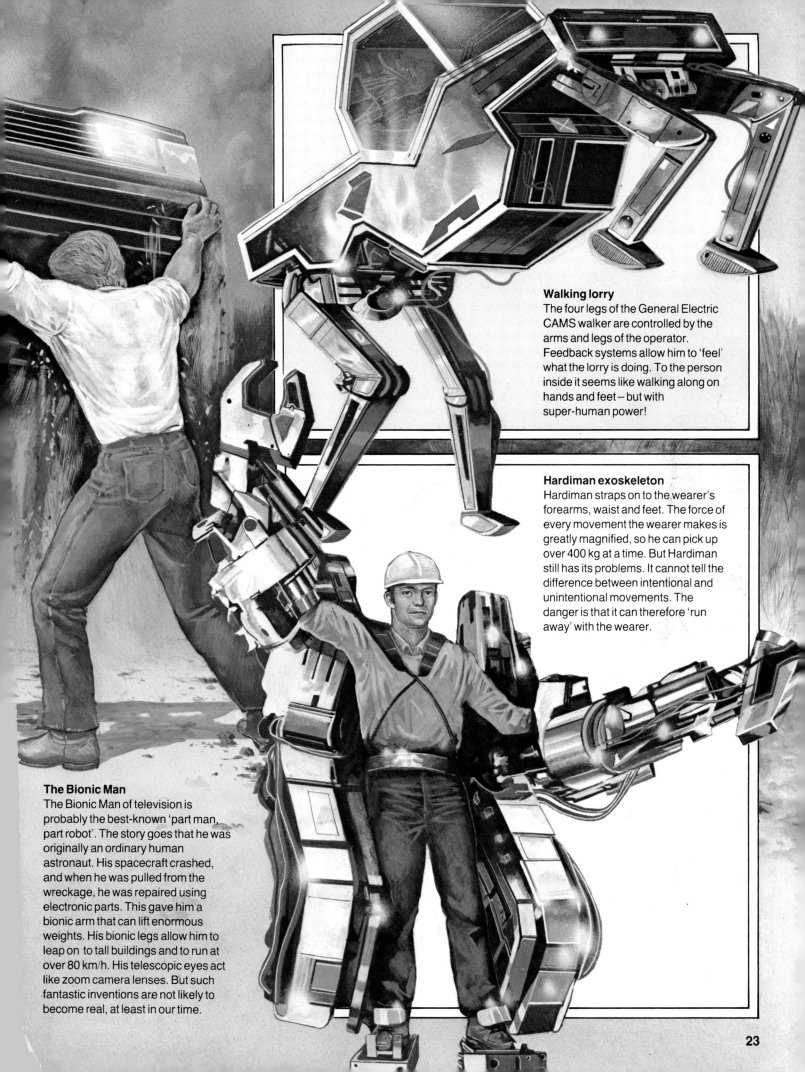

Walking lorry
The four legs of the General Electric CAMS walker are controlled by the arms and legs of the operator. Feedback systems allow him to 'feel' what the lorry is doing. To the person inside it seems like walking along on hands and feet – but with super-human power!

Hardiman exoskeleton
Hardiman straps on to the wearer's forearms, waist and feet. The force of every movement the wearer makes is greatly magnified, so he can pick up over 400 kg at a time. But Hardiman still has its problems. It cannot tell the difference between intentional and unintentional movements. The danger is that it can therefore 'run away' with the wearer.

The Bionic Man
The Bionic Man of television is probably the best-known 'part man, part robot'. The story goes that he was originally an ordinary human astronaut. His spacecraft crashed, and when he was pulled from the wreckage, he was repaired using electronic parts. This gave him a bionic arm that can lift enormous weights. His bionic legs allow him to leap on to tall buildings and to run at over 80 km/h. His telescopic eyes act like zoom camera lenses. But such fantastic inventions are not likely to become real, at least in our time.

23

Robot Film Stars

Film makers and story writers can invent any kind of robot they please. Their stories often take place in the distant future when technology has progressed far beyond our own. Many robots in films and books can think and reason like human beings. Others are gentle helpers with more simple minds. Some are just robot guards or soldiers that mindlessly follow the instructions of their evil masters. One of the earliest film robots was Dr Frankenstein's monster, who was built out of human parts and given life by a charge of electricity. Today's film robots are usually gleaming metal humanoids or androids. One of the reasons that they are so human-like is that they are played by human actors inside the robot costumes. Sometimes, however, film makers use radio-controlled robots, such as R2D2 in *Star Wars* or K9 in *Dr Who*.

Gentle robots

▼ C3PO (or See Threepio) and R2D2 (or Artoo Deetoo) appear in the film *Star Wars*. They are neither stronger nor more intelligent than humans. They are simply gentle slaves who do their jobs as well as they can. Even though they get involved in intergalactic wars, they do not really understand what is happening.

Shiny metal monster

▼ This robot from the television programme *Dr Who* is impressive but obviously not very intelligent. Its sinister, ruthless looks are created by the mask-like face, enormous shoulders and heavy limbs.

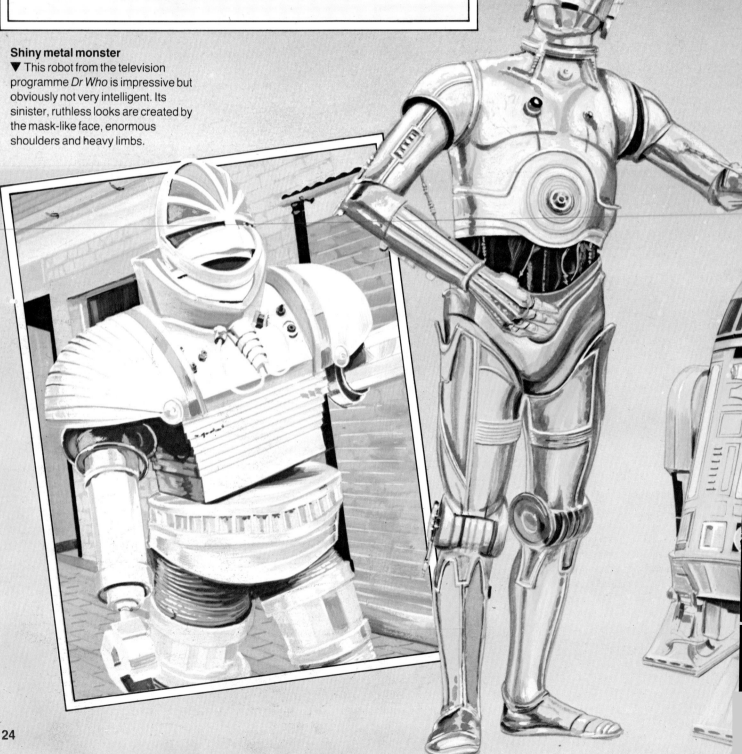

24

Robot repairs
◀ The robots in the film *Westworld* are androids. When they are damaged, they are simply repaired again in secret underground workshops.

Hal, the robot super-brain
▼ In *2001: A Space Odyssey,* the spaceship Discovery I is operated by a Hal 9000 computer. But this is no ordinary computer. Hal thinks, talks, hears and even lip-reads. He is a super-intelligent robot brain. Hal decides that he does not need the human crew and he kills all of them except one. However, this sole survivor manages to destroy most of Hal's brain, leaving only the part that keeps the spaceship going.

Experimental Robots

Some robots in films can think and do extremely complicated things, but it will be a long time before this happens in real life. Present-day robots have to 'know' a considerable amount before they can carry out even simple tasks. They have to be programmed with a great deal of information before being set to work. However, scientists are trying to create true robot brains that can 'think' for themselves. They will be able to learn by experience and use logic to work out problems just as humans do. Scientists have already developed computer systems which are expert in particular subjects. One such system helps geologists to search for oil. Another helps doctors find out what is wrong with their patients. Computer scientists are now trying to develop a system that will help solve problems in any subject.

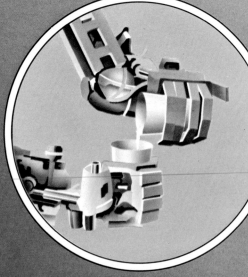

Sensitive hands
WABOT-1 has eight sensors on each hand which provide feedback information for his computer brain. The brain sends instructions to the hands to hold objects with just enough pressure to stop them falling – too much pressure might crush delicate things. WABOT-1 is shown above pouring water from one glass to another.

A robot that walks and talks
WABOT-1 can make simple decisions. He can be told to pick up an object and take it to another place. First he replies that he will carry out the task. Then he looks for the object with his cameras, measures how far away it is and walks towards it. He stops, picks up the object and takes it to the right place.

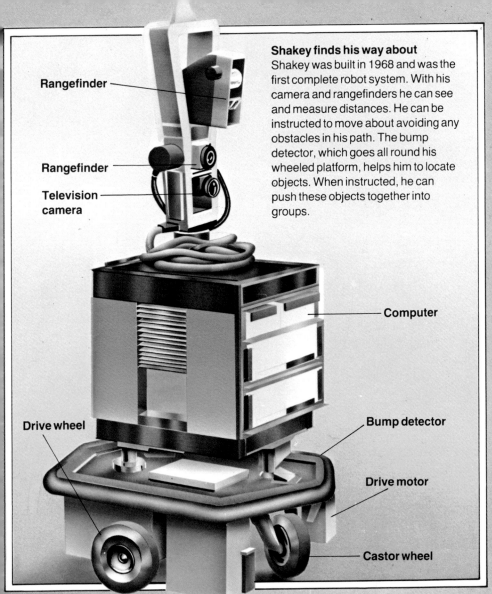

Shakey finds his way about

Shakey was built in 1968 and was the first complete robot system. With his camera and rangefinders he can see and measure distances. He can be instructed to move about avoiding any obstacles in his path. The bump detector, which goes all round his wheeled platform, helps him to locate objects. When instructed, he can push these objects together into groups.

Rangefinder

Rangefinder

Television camera

Computer

Drive wheel

Bump detector

Drive motor

Castor wheel

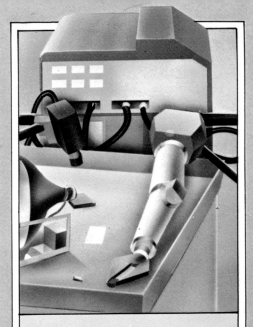

Robots that can see and think

Industrial assembly robots are already being used to put small parts together. But the parts must be given to these assembly robots in a precise order. Engineers are now building assembly robots with television camera 'eyes'. Such a robot will be able to select the parts it needs from a tray and then put them together correctly all by itself.

Feeling by remote control

Scientists have developed a remote-controlled robot arm that copies the exact movements of someone operating an identical arm. It may soon be possible to use this system in space. The operator will remain on Earth, watching a television screen. Meanwhile, a robot slave arm, attached to a spacecraft, will be working in space. The operator will be able to 'feel' what the robot arm is touching through tiny air-jets.

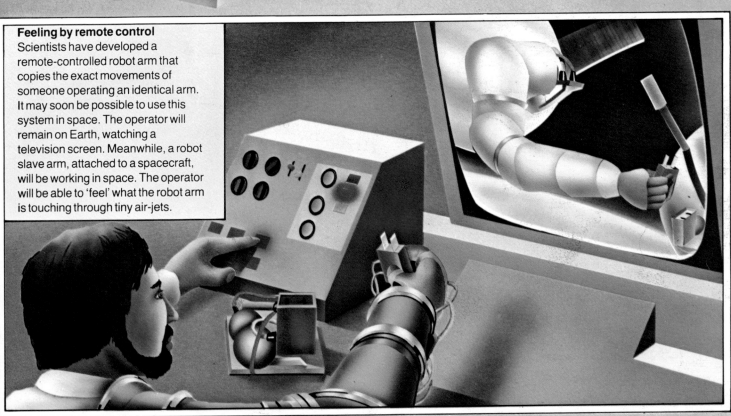

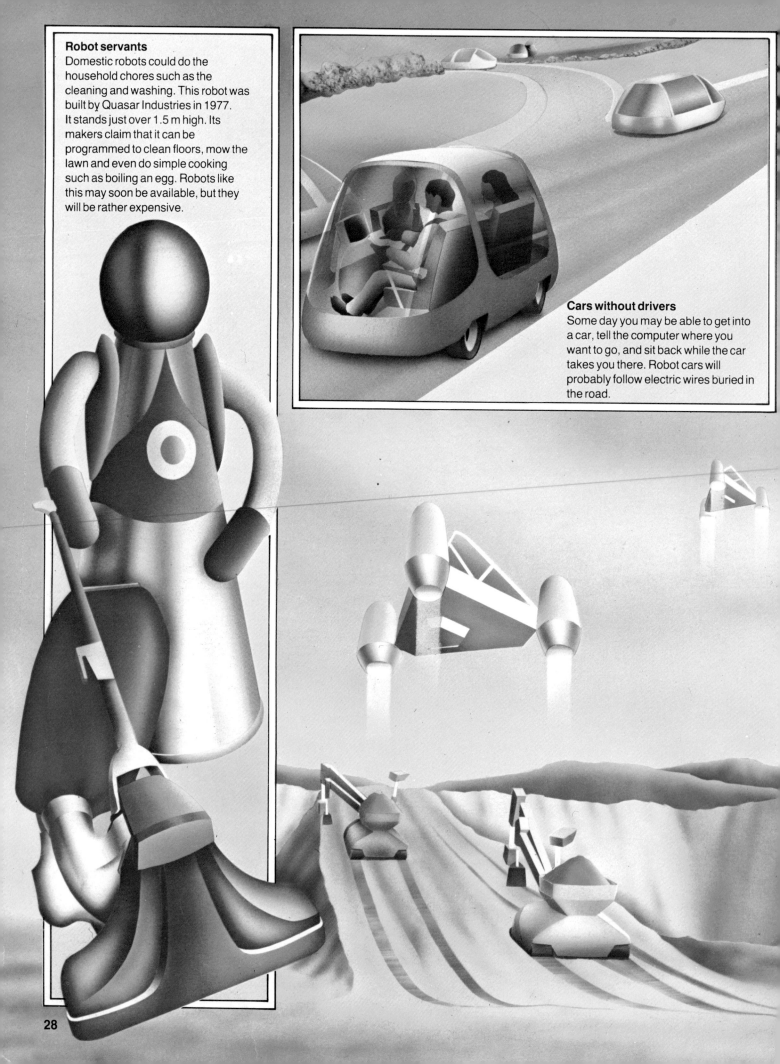

Robot servants
Domestic robots could do the household chores such as the cleaning and washing. This robot was built by Quasar Industries in 1977. It stands just over 1.5 m high. Its makers claim that it can be programmed to clean floors, mow the lawn and even do simple cooking such as boiling an egg. Robots like this may soon be available, but they will be rather expensive.

Cars without drivers
Some day you may be able to get into a car, tell the computer where you want to go, and sit back while the car takes you there. Robot cars will probably follow electric wires buried in the road.

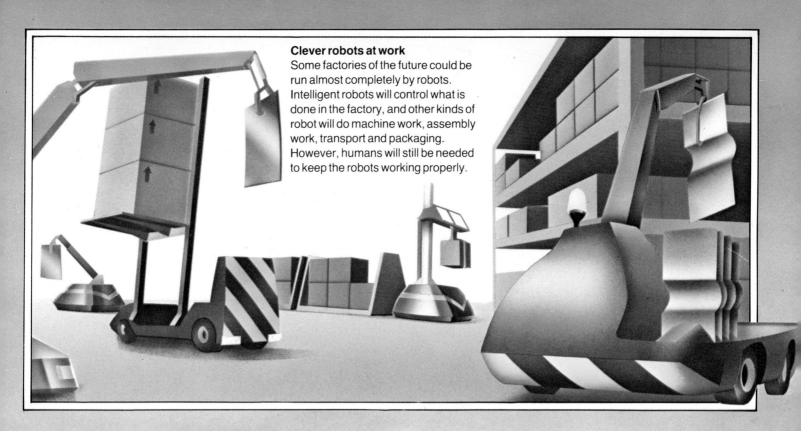

Clever robots at work

Some factories of the future could be run almost completely by robots. Intelligent robots will control what is done in the factory, and other kinds of robot will do machine work, assembly work, transport and packaging. However, humans will still be needed to keep the robots working properly.

Robots in the Future

We already have robots that can see, hear and feel; they use cameras, microphones and touch sensors. Some robots can even speak, using electronic devices called speech synthesizers. In this age of the silicon chip it is certain that robots with better and better brains will be developed. In the future scientists will develop domestic robots, robot cars, intelligent industrial robots, robot space shuttles and many others. There are also lots of possibilities for remote-controlled machines. For example, imagine a complete slave robot exploring an unknown planet. The slave could send back touch, sight, hearing, taste and smell information, and the human operator on earth would feel exactly as if he was on the surface of the planet.

Mining other worlds

Robots will continue to be very important in space exploration because they do not need life-support systems, and they can be built to withstand extreme heat or extreme cold. On distant planets robot explorers may one day discover valuable minerals. It might be possible to use robot miners to dig out these mineral ores, and robot spacecraft to bring them back to Earth.

In America, Grumman Aerospace Corporation have already designed a robot beam builder. It will be used in building space stations. Robot shuttles will deliver materials to stations being built out in space.

Some useful words

Android A robot that looks exactly like a human being.

Anthropomorphous Having human-like qualities.

Automatic Working by itself, without direct human control.

Automaton An automatic machine that imitates a human being or other living thing.

Bionic device An electronic copy of part of a living organism. The word 'bionic' comes from BIOlogical and electroNIC.

CAMS Cybernetic Anthropomorphous Machine Systems – robot systems devised by General Electric, USA.

Computer An electronic machine that makes rapid calculations and processes information.

Computer system A computer and its program or sequence of programs.

Cybernetics The study of control and communication systems, particularly in machines that control themselves.

Cyborg A robot that is part man and part machine.

Electronic device A piece of electrical equipment that contains transistors.

Feedback Information about changes in the output of a system that is transmitted back to the system, and used to control the system itself.

Input data Information put into a computer. This can be done using magnetic tape, holes punched in cards, or holes punched in paper tape. The computer brains of some robots also receive input data from touch sensors, cameras and microphones.

Program Instructions given to a computer that tell it what to do with the input data.

Robot A machine that is human-like, either in appearance or in its actions. A true robot controls itself. It has a computer brain and feedback systems.

Robotics The study of robots.

Silicon chip A tiny piece of silicon on which there is a complex electronic circuit.

Transistor A device that controls the flow of current in an electrical circuit.

More About Robots

There are many stories and films about robots, but the study of real robots has not been going on for very long. As a result, there are few books about modern robots, and few places where you can go and see robots. Unfortunately, many firms that use industrial robots keep them secret. As time goes on, however, more and more information about robots will become available. Meanwhile you can have fun finding out as much as you can. Look out for items in newspapers and magazines about new and more advanced robots. You could also try building the do-it-yourself robot suit shown here. Or you can design your own model robot using odds and ends, from cardboard boxes to old sweet cartons, that you might find in and around your home.

Make a robot suit

This robot costume is made from all sorts of odds and ends. The body is made from a large cardboard box. The head is another box with a plastic colander on top (half a plastic ball would do instead). The arms and legs are made of cardboard tubes.

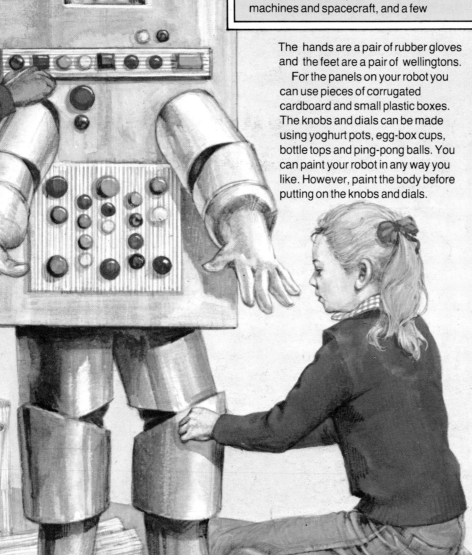

Finding out more

The British Robot Association was formed in 1978 to help promote the use of robots in industry. If you would like to know more about industrial robots write to:
The British Robot Association,
35-39 High Street,
Kempston,
Bedford MK42 7BT.
They will tell you if there are any industrial robots in your area that you can go and see. They will also provide information about new developments.

Books to read

An excellent inexpensive book to look out for is *How it Works . . . The Computer* by David Carey, published by Ladybird Books. It describes how computers work and what they do. There are also many books on war machines and spacecraft, and a few very advanced books on robots and cybernetics.

The best known books about robots are stories. Try *I, Robot* and *The Rest of the Robots* by Isaac Asimov, published by Panther Books. These are books of short stories, written for adults, about robots in the distant future.

Films

Frankenstein (1931), Universal. This is only one of over 40 films about Frankenstein's monster.
Tobor the Great (1954), Republic.
Target Earth (1954), Allied Artists.
Gog (1954), Ivan Tors.
Forbidden Planet (1956), MGM.
2001: A Space Odyssey (1968), MGM.
Silent Running (1971), Universal.
Westworld (1973), MGM.
Logan's Run (1976), MGM.
Star Wars (1977), Lucasfilm.
The Empire Strikes Back (1980), Lucasfilm.

The hands are a pair of rubber gloves and the feet are a pair of wellingtons.

For the panels on your robot you can use pieces of corrugated cardboard and small plastic boxes. The knobs and dials can be made using yoghurt pots, egg-box cups, bottle tops and ping-pong balls. You can paint your robot in any way you like. However, paint the body before putting on the knobs and dials.

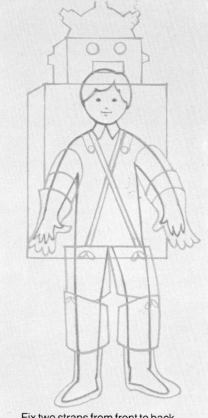

Fix two straps from front to back inside the robot body. Position them so that they rest comfortably on the wearer's shoulders. Make sure that the wearer can see out of the opening. The legs can be supported by a pair of braces. The lower parts of the legs are fixed loosely to the upper parts with string.